AF599105

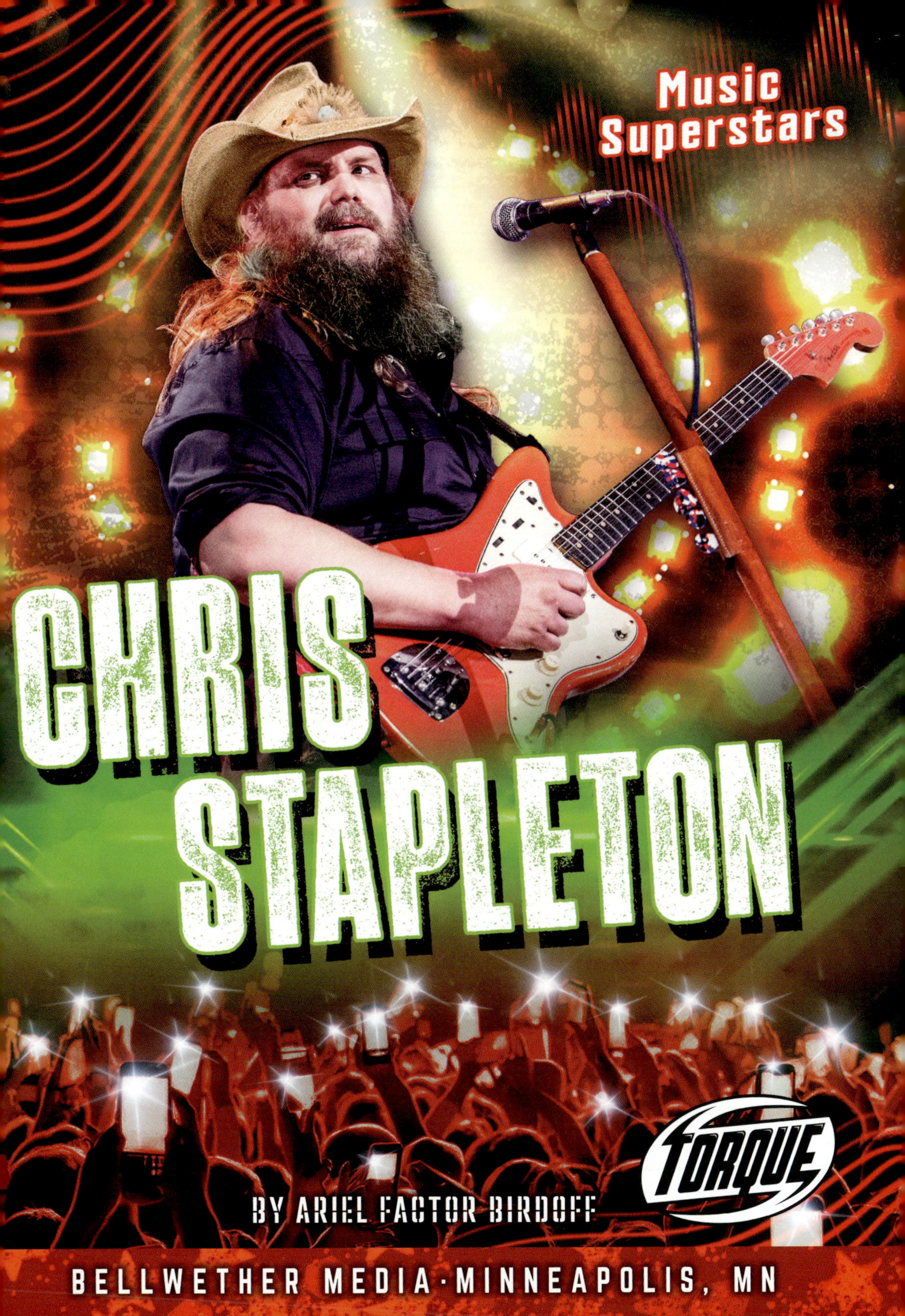
Music Superstars
CHRIS STAPLETON
BY ARIEL FACTOR BIRDOFF
TORQUE
BELLWETHER MEDIA·MINNEAPOLIS, MN

Torque brims with excitement
perfect for thrill-seekers of all kinds.
Discover daring survival skills, explore
uncharted worlds, and marvel at mighty
engines and extreme sports. In *Torque* books,
anything can happen. Are you ready?

This edition first published in 2025 by Bellwether Media, Inc.

Library of Congress Cataloging-in-Publication Data

Names: Birdoff, Ariel Factor, author.
Title: Chris Stapleton / by Ariel Factor Birdoff.
Description: Minneapolis, MN : Bellwether Media, 2025. | Series: Music superstars | Includes bibliographical references and index. | Audience: Ages 7-12 | Audience: Grades 4-6 | Summary: "Engaging images accompany information about Chris Stapleton. The combination of high-interest subject matter and light text is intended for students in grades 3 through 7"– Provided by publisher.
Identifiers: LCCN 2024046994 (print) | LCCN 2024046995 (ebook) | ISBN 9798893042641 (library binding) | ISBN 9798893043617 (ebook)
Subjects: LCSH: Stapleton, Chris, 1978–Juvenile literature. | Country musicians–United States–Biography–Juvenile literature. | LCGFT: Biographies.
Classification: LCC ML3930.S73 B57 2025 (print) | LCC ML3930.S73 (ebook) | DDC 782.421642092 [B]–dc23/eng/20241008
LC record available at https://lccn.loc.gov/2024046994
LC ebook record available at https://lccn.loc.gov/2024046995

Editor: Elizabeth Neuenfeldt   Designer: Josh Brink

Printed in the United States of America, North Mankato, MN.

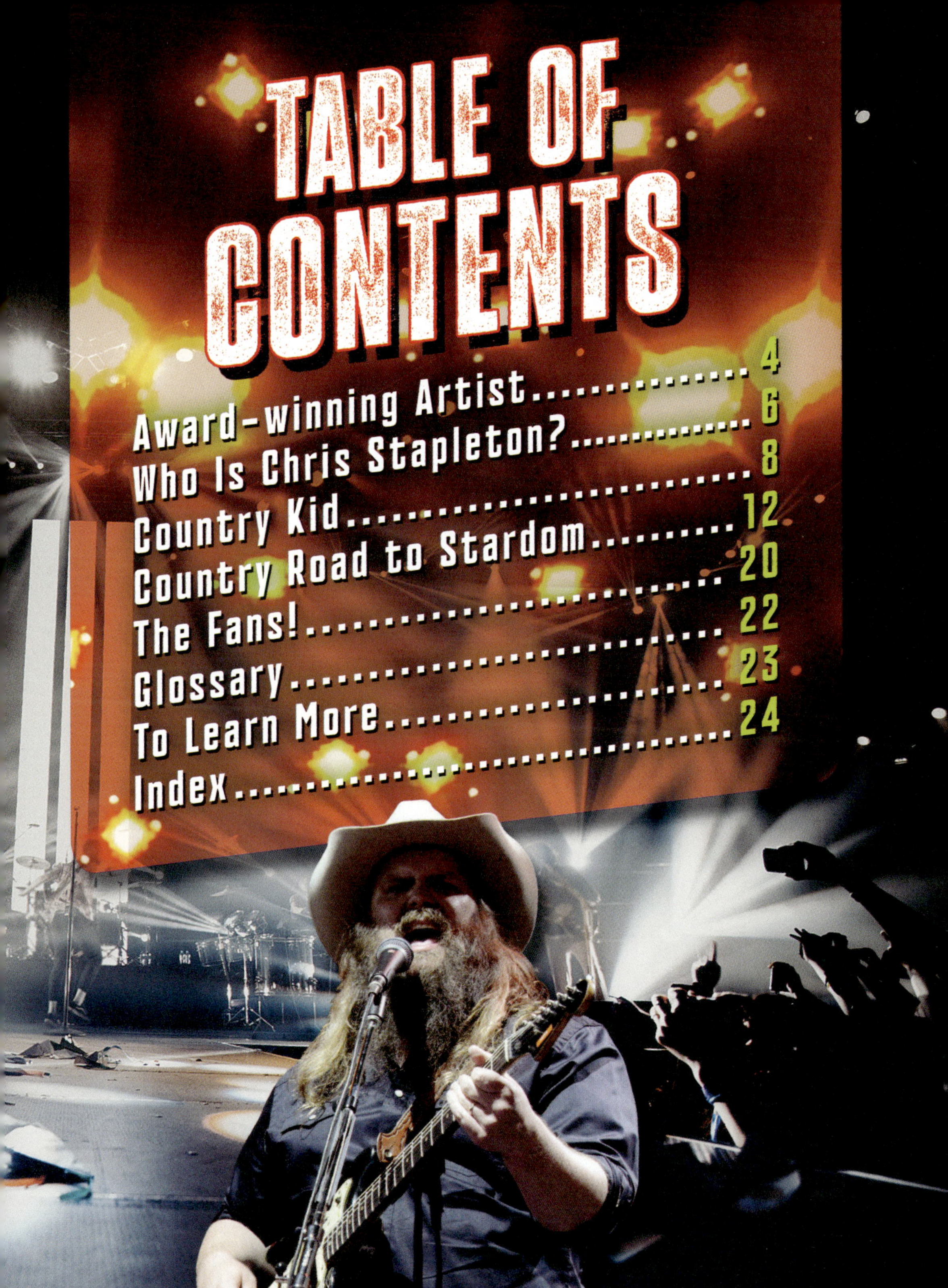

TABLE OF CONTENTS

AWARD-WINNING ARTIST

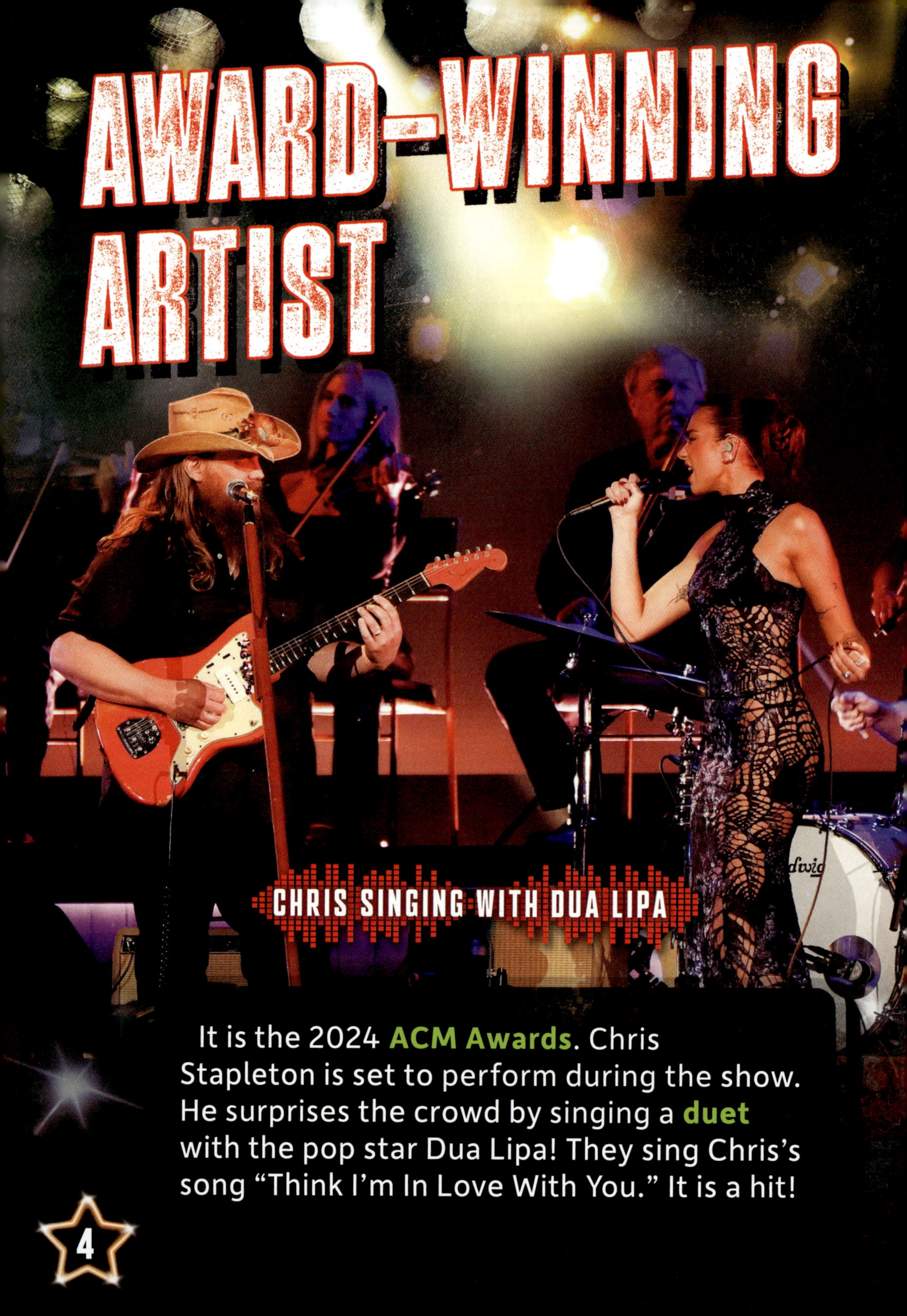

CHRIS SINGING WITH DUA LIPA

It is the 2024 **ACM Awards**. Chris Stapleton is set to perform during the show. He surprises the crowd by singing a **duet** with the pop star Dua Lipa! They sing Chris's song "Think I'm In Love With You." It is a hit!

The same night, Chris wins four ACM Awards. He is a music superstar!

WHO IS CHRIS STAPLETON?

Christopher "Chris" Alvin Stapleton is an American country music singer and songwriter. He plays the guitar, too!

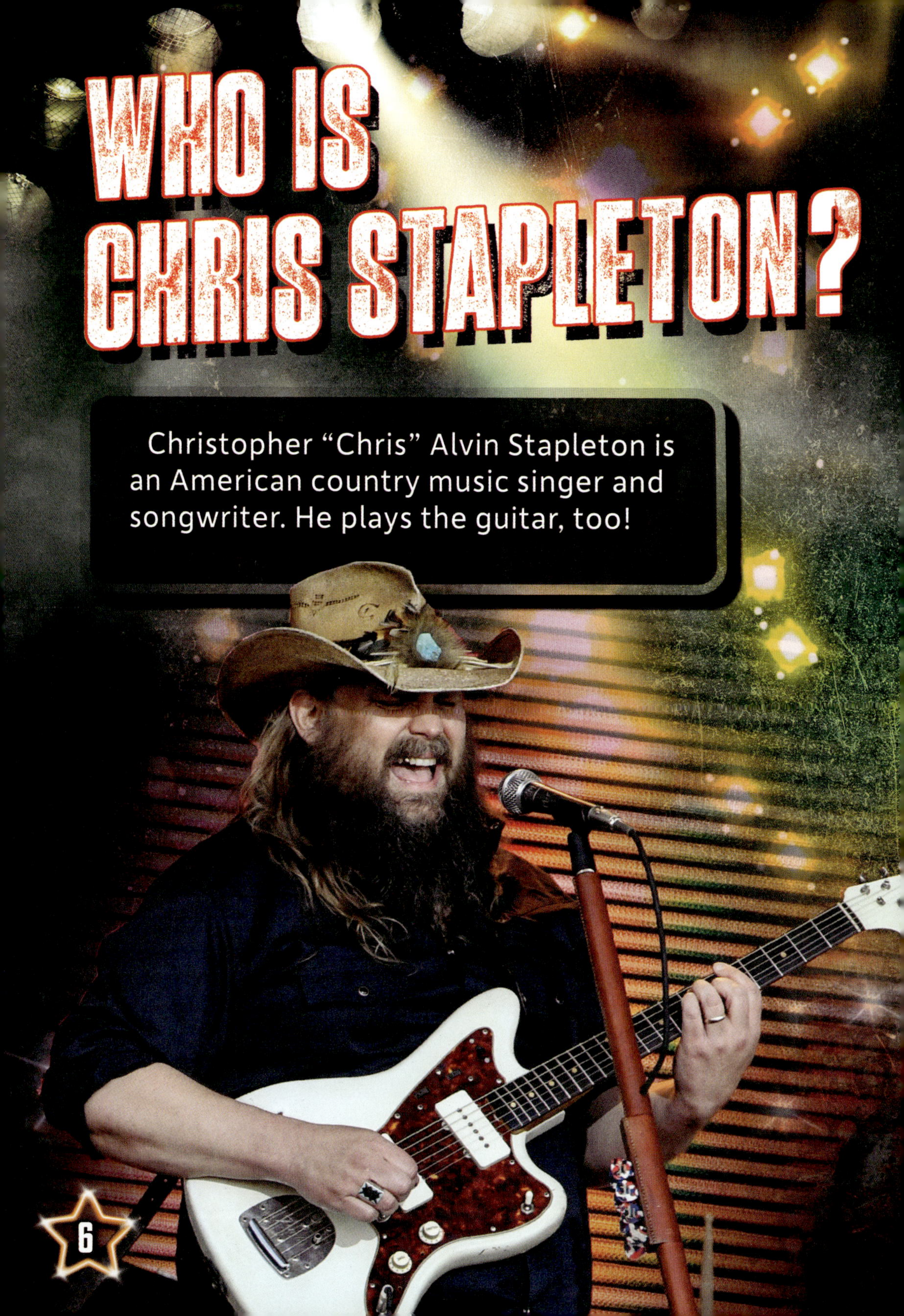

CHRIS STAPLETON

Birthday
April 15, 1978

Hometown
Lexington, Kentucky

Types of Music
country, southern rock, bluegrass

First Solo Hit
"Tennessee Whiskey"

Before he became a **solo** artist, Chris wrote songs for other country singers. He also sang in two different bands. Now, Chris has won many awards. He is one of the best country music artists in the world!

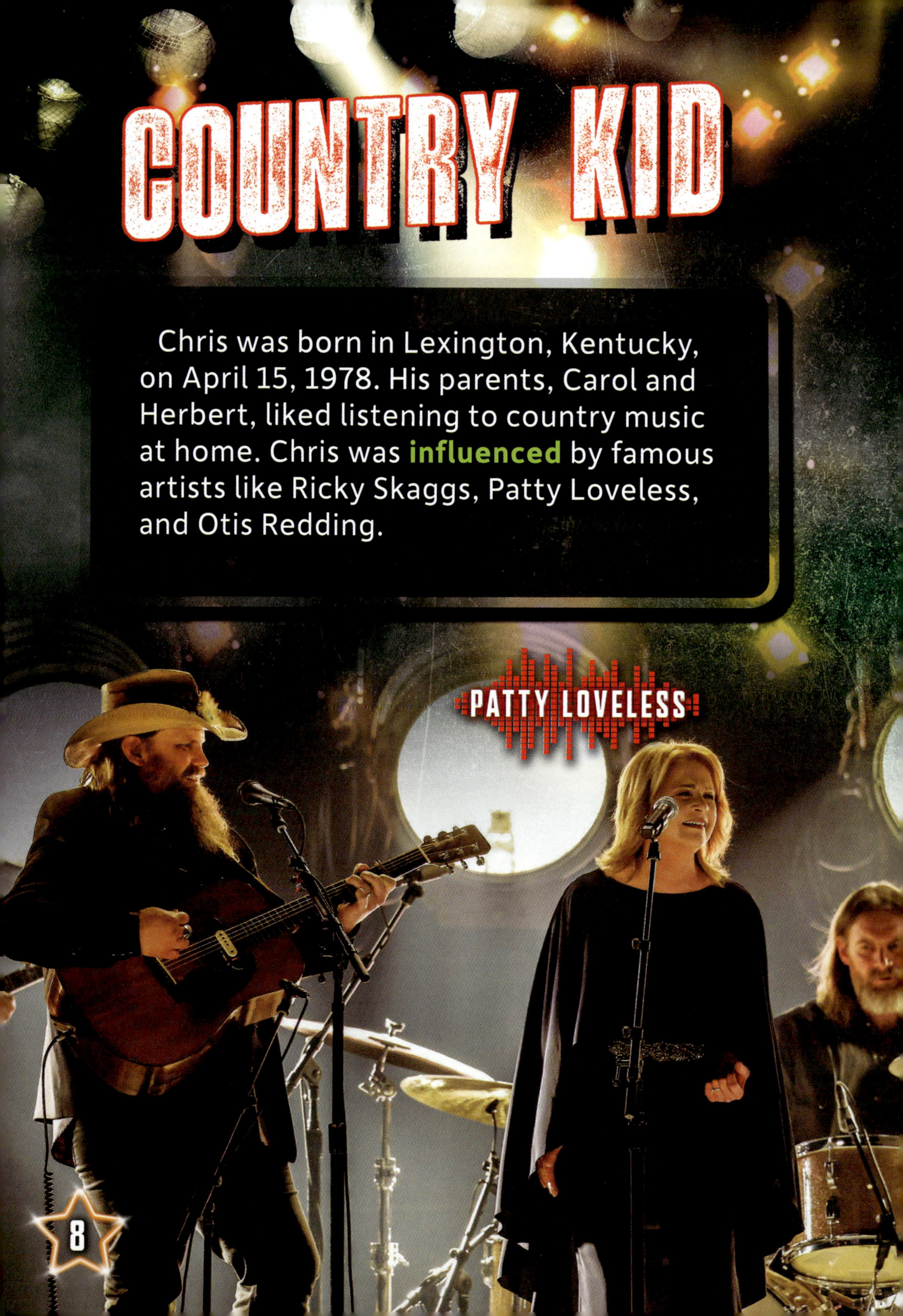

COUNTRY KID

Chris was born in Lexington, Kentucky, on April 15, 1978. His parents, Carol and Herbert, liked listening to country music at home. Chris was **influenced** by famous artists like Ricky Skaggs, Patty Loveless, and Otis Redding.

PATTY LOVELESS

GIVING BACK

In 2016, Chris performed at his former high school. He also gave $57,000 worth of musical instruments to the school!

Besides country music, Chris loved sports. He played on his high school's football team.

Chris finished high school as **valedictorian**. Afterwards, he went to college in Tennessee to study engineering. Later, Chris decided to make music instead. He left school.

In 2001, he moved to Nashville. He signed a **contract** with Sea Gayle Music. Chris's country music career had begun!

COUNTRY ROAD TO STARDOM

TIM MCGRAW AND KENNY CHESNEY

Chris was a songwriter first. He wrote country hits for Kenny Chesney, Lee Ann Womack, Tim McGraw, and more!

Chris also played in bands. In 2006, he joined the SteelDrivers. They **released** two albums that were **nominated** for **Grammy Awards**. He later released one album with another band called the Jompson Brothers.

PLAYING MANY PARTS

While in the SteelDrivers, Chris was the lead singer, guitarist, and songwriter!

In 2013, Chris signed with Mercury Nashville Records. He had started his career as a solo artist. Shortly after, he released his first single, "What Are You Listening To?"

Then, Chris began working on his first solo album. He decided to work with his wife, Morgane. As a songwriter herself, Morgane helped Chris pick the perfect songs.

CHRIS AND MORGANE STAPLETON

Traveller was released in 2015. Later, at that year's **CMA Awards**, *Traveller* won Album of the Year. Chris also won Male Vocalist of the Year and New Artist of the Year!

At the **ceremony**, Chris sang a duet with pop star Justin Timberlake. Chris Stapleton had officially become a country music star!

10 Grammy Awards

15 ACM Awards Awards

16 CMA Awards

5 *Billboard* Music Awards

TRAVELING TO THE GRAMMYS

Traveller won Best

In 2017, Chris released *From A Room: Volume 1* and *Volume 2*. *Volume 1* later won Album of the Year at the CMA Awards. It also won a Grammy for Best Country Album!

His album *Higher* came out in 2023. It was number one on the ***Billboard*** Top Country Albums list. Chris continues to be a number one artist in country music!

TIMELINE

– 2013 –
Chris begins his solo career

– 2015 –
Chris releases the album *Traveller*

– 2016–
Chris wins his first Grammy Award

SUPER BOWL SINGER
In 2023, Chris sang the United States national anthem at Super Bowl LVII!
CHRIS SINGING AT SUPER BOWL LVII
–2017–
Chris releases the albums *From a Room: Volume 1* and *Volume 2*
CHRIS STAPLETON
–2023–
Chris sings the national anthem at Super Bowl LVII

THE FANS!

Whether he is writing or performing, Chris Stapleton has many fans. He has sold out concerts in countries around the world! Chris's fans appreciate **authentic** and moving music straight from the heart.

PLAYLIST

"Tennessee Whiskey"
(2015)

"Broken Halos"
(2017)

"You Should Probably Leave"
(2020)

"Think I'm In Love With You"
(2023)

"White Horse"
(2023)

Chris Stapleton was raised on country music. He has now become one of its most celebrated stars!

GLOSSARY

ACM Awards—a yearly event during which awards are given for achievements in country music; ACM stands for Academy of Country Music.

authentic—real

Billboard—related to a well-known music news magazine and website that ranks songs and albums

ceremony—a formal event for presenting awards

CMA Awards—a yearly event during which awards are presented for achievements in country music; CMA stands for Country Music Association.

contract—an agreement between two or more people

duet—a song performed by two people

Grammy Awards—yearly awards given by the Recording Academy of the United States for achievements in music; Grammy Awards are also called Grammys.

influenced—affected by

nominated—chosen as a candidate for an award

released—made a song available for listening

solo—relating to music performed by one person

valedictorian—the highest ranked student in a graduating class

TO LEARN MORE

AT THE LIBRARY

Nguyen, Suzane. *Taylor Swift*. Minneapolis, Minn.: Bellwether Media, 2025.

Richards, Mary, and David Schweitzer. *A History of Music for Children*. New York, N.Y.: Thames & Hudson, 2021.

Whitaker, Chelsea. *Chris Stapleton*. Broomall, Pa.: Mason Crest, 2021.

ON THE WEB

FACTSURFER

Factsurfer.com gives you a safe, fun way to find more information.

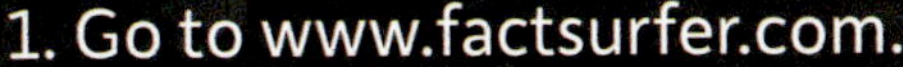

1. Go to www.factsurfer.com.
2. Enter “Chris Stapleton” into the search box and click 🔍.
3. Select your book cover to see a list of related content.

INDEX

The images in this book are reproduced through the courtesy of: John Shearer/ Getty Images, front cover, p. 9; Catsense, front cover (lights); Taya Ovod, pp. 2-3; Adam McCullough, p. 3; Chris Pizzello/ Invision/ AP Newsroom, pp. 4-5, 16; Eyepix/ NurPhoto/ AP Newsroom, p. 5; PG/ Bauer-Griffin/ Getty Images, p. 6; Jason Davis/ Stringer/ Getty Images, p. 7; WENN/ Alamy, p. 7 (infographic); UPI/ Alamy, pp. 8-9; ZUMA Press/ Alamy, p. 10; Missmojorising/ Wikipedia, p. 11; Dylanhatfield, p. 11 (cowboy boots); jbrink, pp. 11 (Tom Petty album), 18-19 (albums), 21 (playlist); Dejan Lazarevic, p. 11 (cowboy hat); LBJ Library/ Wikipedia, p. 11 (Gibson); Kevin Winter/ ACMA2012/ Getty Images, pp. 12-13; Michael Loccisano/ FilmMagic/ Getty Images, p. 13; Gary Miller/ WireImage/ Getty Images, p. 14; Amy Harris/ Invision/ AP Newsroom, pp. 14-15; CarlosVdeHabsburgo/ Wikipedia, pp. 17 (Grammy Awards), 18 (Grammy Awards); Amy Nichole Harris, p. 17 (ACM Awards); s_bukley, p. 17 (CMA Awards); Kathy Hutchins, p. 17 (*Billboard* Music Awards); Kevin Mazur/ Getty Images, pp. 18-19; Dabarti CGI, pp. 18-19 (timeline mixing board); Casey Brooke Lawson/ Invision/ AP Newsroom, p. 20; SUZANNE CORDEIRO/ AFP/ Getty Images, p. 21; Debby Wong, p. 23.